HOW WE
SUCCEED

MAKING GOOD THINGS HAPPEN THROUGH THE
POWER OF SMART EXPERIMENTS

DEDICATED TO ALL MY BEST TEACHERS:
RUTH, HAROLD, IDA, DEB, HENRY, JENNY

How We Succeed

Making Good Things Happen Through the Power of Smart Experiments

By Steven K. Gold

Published in the United States of America by 1776 Ventures.

For information about special discounts for bulk purchases of the book, please contact the publisher directly at publisher@wesucceed.org.

To inquire about speaking engagements for the author or individuals profiled, contact our representative at speakers@wesucceed.org.

Special thanks to Carol Fazio for the design of the book, Albert Ganss for the illustrations, and Mihaela Drakulovic for the cover art.

Printed in the United States of America

ISBN 978-0-692-54631-4

www.stevenkgold.com

CONTENTS

THE MISSION

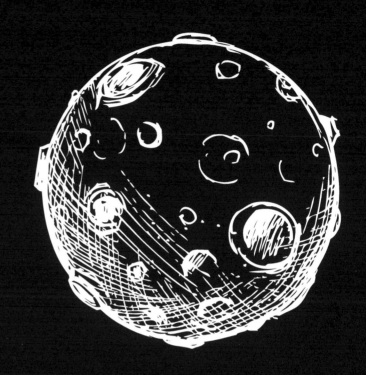

THE BEST JOURNEYS ANSWER QUESTIONS
THAT AT THE BEGINNING,
YOU DIDN'T EVEN THINK TO ASK.

180° South

Have you ever wondered why some people succeed more than others? How do they manage to achieve so much, so consistently over the long run? Is there some special combination of factors that propel them forward?

For more than twenty years, my research has explored the critical factors that contribute to a person's ability to sustainably achieve and succeed more—the behaviors that differentiate high achievers from everyone else.

So what are the critical factors? It turns out that there are three primary ones. Let's call these the building blocks of sustainable success:

Experiments are investments of resources that allow us to discover how the world works. They empower us to build a bridge to an uncertain future. They're the focus of this book and in the next several chapters we'll learn about Smart Experiments and how to do them well.

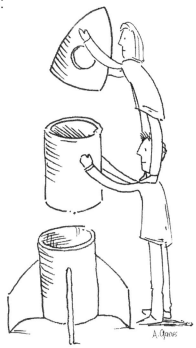

Relationships are our ongoing connections with others. Constantly creating and strengthening relationships is another key to long-term achievement and success.

Expertise means being able to do one or more things really well. In the best case we perform better than everyone else. We earn expertise through hard work, education, practice and real world experience.

These three building blocks are interdependent. We use experiments to explore relationships and build expertise. Relationships, on the other hand, are leveraged in our experiments and used to gain expertise. Finally, expertise is something that helps us to do our experiments and strengthen our relationships. *How We Succeed* focuses on how we can do the best **experiments**—meaning how we can wisely invest our resources to *discover and acquire more value for ourselves and others*.

Experiments come in all shapes and sizes.

Some experiments are trivial, like walking across a room. We wouldn't normally give much thought to such a simple act, despite the fact that it involves some investment (of time and energy at a minimum) and has an outcome that isn't completely predictable. For example, how often have you been sidetracked walking through the office or your home? Other experiments are medium-sized. What happens when I meet this friend or that client? Do I take the busy highway or the slower back roads? Will eating this food keep me up tonight? These are examples of the small experiments we do throughout the day.

Then we have the big experiments. These are major investments of resources to, for example, attend a certain school, choose a career path, take a new job, or marry the love of one's life. These are just a few examples of high-impact experiments where the outcomes will have a major effect on a person's life. In exactly the same way, organizations undertake all kinds of experiments. For example, businesses are started, acquired, merged and sold; people get hired and fired, all kinds of things are manufactured, marketed and transacted; partnerships are made, and lots more. Individuals and organizations that make good things happen have experiments—of all shapes and sizes—at their core.

LIFE IS A SERIES OF EXPERIMENTS

This idea that our lives are filled with experiments will benefit from examples. To demonstrate the point I decided to jot down notes about some of the many experiments being done by my family and friends during a typical weekday.

6:30am Time to wake the kids up so they can get ready for school. My wife enters our room announcing that she did an experiment this morning to get them out of bed. She had received an email with photos of newborn twins in the family and decided to test if this new and valuable information could rouse our daughter. The screams of excitement that ensued also got our son out of bed. Wonderful!

6:55am Our son, up and dressed earlier than usual, announces he wants to make poached eggs. This isn't a normal experiment most mornings (or for most people), but I told him to go for it. He invested his newfound time, lots of enthusiasm, a few eggs and his ego in the experiment. The water boiled over and congealed on the stovetop, the egg whites glued themselves to the bottom of the pot, and his ego was burst for the moment. Fortunately a bowl of cereal got him on his way.

7:41am Our kids' teachers are always doing experiments. On the drive to school, my daughter tells me about the dead raccoon in the school parking lot and how her teacher took the entire class out to observe it and then write a poem about it. What a brilliant and beautiful experiment that inspired the class to learn and create.

8:12am I talk with a friend who's in the construction business. He tells me about a massive international project that his company is pursuing. It's a textbook example of doing a series of experiments. They've invested their own resources to develop relationships, create site plans, and deal with partners and investors. They are doing one smart experiment after another in an effort to transform a dream into reality.

8:45am With a few hours before my next commitment I can work on this book. Today I'm sketching out graphics to share with my designer. Is this an experiment? Of course! I'm investing my energy and expertise to create a concept that I'll share with her. Will she understand my doodles? Sure. Will she laugh at them and poke fun at me? Probably. Will they fit into the book in a way that works? Hope so!

1:00pm An investor calls and tells me that he's looking for new opportunities. I put two and two together and decide to do an experiment. I create an Executive Summary for a new venture that makes use of several available resources: an idea, patents I have, possible co-founders, etc. I'm an opportunist and it's an experiment with no downside. If he's interested, great. If not, I've got plenty on my 'to do' list.

4:25pm Since I'm working at home today my daughter comes up as soon as she's home from school. She's excited because she learned that she'll be able to sell her crafts at her school's holiday fair. She's got the entrepreneurial gene and she's ready to kick into gear. Of course it's all an experiment. Will her investment of time and materials (that she purchased with her own money) work out? Will people buy her crafts? Will she make a profit? No matter what happens I know she'll learn a lot.

6:30pm My wife arrives home and discovers that the leftovers intended for dinner have been eaten (by me, I was hungry). She gathers up some available ingredients and—investing both her calm demeanor and expertise—cooks up a great dinner.

7:45pm I told my son that I'd play chess with him after he finished his homework. Chess is a series of experiments, with each move of a piece prompting a reply from the other player. Each move informs the next move as our experiments and their outcomes come to light. We end the night with each of us winning a game.

As you can see from these examples, our experiments relate to everything we do. Whether we're playing games or building skyscrapers, we're doing experiments.

My life's quest to discover why some people and organizations succeed much more than others began quite a few years ago. It all started with my studies of psychology and organizational behavior in college, continued in medical school, intensified during my decades as an entrepreneur seeking and finding my own success, and is now the driving force of my current activities advising entrepreneurs, executives and government officials around the world. Since entrepreneurs are some of the best people to study when it comes to succeeding and failing, my research also included the full-time observation (all day every day for 10 weeks at a time) of 84 entrepreneurs as they pursued their dreams. All of these experiences and relationships have given me a front-row seat to the ways that we think, behave, fail and succeed—and the factors that predispose us to sustainably achieve and succeed more in our lives.

★

PEOPLE AND ORGANIZATIONS THAT MAKE THINGS HAPPEN ALL HAVE EXPERIMENTATION AT THEIR CORE.

As a result, this book is unique. First, my findings are not based on anecdotal evidence or upbeat success stories. That approach works well for headlines and bestsellers, but it misses the point and doesn't allow us to discover the real insights. Instead, the approach I've taken is to look at the behaviors and outcomes for both high achievers and low achievers. Another way of saying this is that I've conducted a placebo-controlled prospective study (of sorts) of human success—similar to the method that's used by pharmaceutical companies to test if new drugs work.

There's an important reason why any study of how we succeed should be done in this way. If we look at success stories alone, then we'll never really know how high achievers behave in contrast to low achievers. Another way of saying this is that people who succeed more and people who succeed less behave in many of the same ways, which doesn't help us to isolate the unique factors that drive consistent long-term achievement and success. Platitudes such as work hard, get grit, learn from failure, etc. just aren't helpful. By observing a wide range of individuals and organizations as they succeed and fail in all kinds of situations, I've discovered behaviors that empower high achievers to sustainably succeed more and uncovered nuances that don't emerge in most success narratives.

As the quote at the start of this chapter reminds us, our journeys have a way of taking on lives of their own. In particular, I've been compelled to question the meaning of commonly used words—such as 'succeeding' and 'success'—and to seek clear definitions for them. I'll share my definitions soon, but for now it's enough to say that clear definitions for these words will allow us to have a much more meaningful discussion about succeeding over the long run.

How We Succeed is also different from other books of its kind by being solidly grounded in the science of human behavior. While we all enjoy a good story, and I include a few stories in this book, anecdotes often mislead us. They gloss over the less-exciting details and subtleties of success-oriented behavior, and all too often focus on people who have benefited more from luck than their deliberate actions. In fact, while most highly successful people create fascinating narratives (especially when they write biographies or have others write them on their behalf), they're rarely able to explain their own behavior, let alone the specific behaviors that were crucial to their success. This book is based on more than twenty years of academic and practical research in the realms of biology, neurophysiology, organizational behavior, systems engineering, finance and economics, logic and game theory, and more. *How We Succeed* offers something beyond anecdotes;

MY MISSION IS SIMPLE: TO SHARE SMART EXPERIMENTS IN A WAY THAT EMPOWERS ALL OF US TO ACHIEVE AND SUCCEED MORE IN OUR LIVES.

it presents a valuable method to be used by individuals and organizations engaged in all kinds of activities. No matter what we're up to, doing our experiments well empowers us to achieve and succeed more.

How We Succeed teaches us about **Smart Experiments**. As we now realize, all of us do experiments all of the time. This is how we discover and accumulate value for ourselves and others. We'll soon see, however, that not all experiments are created equal. Some experiments are better than others in the same way that any process can be done poorly or well. Not all conversations, heart surgeries, political forays, chess games, mergers and acquisitions, product and rocket launches, etc. are of the same quality or lead to the best outcomes. Smart Experiments offer us a simple and powerful method that predisposes to better outcomes on average. This doesn't mean that every outcome will be positive or predictable, but it does mean that most outcomes will allow us to accumulate value and do even bigger and more meaningful experiments over time.

My mission is simple: to share Smart Experiments in a way that empowers all of us—individuals and organizations—to achieve and succeed more in our lives.

PREPARE TO LAUNCH

 Life has its defining moments. During the writing of this book, such a moment occurred when I realized that I needed to share some definitions. Fortunately, this was familiar territory. It took me back to the time when, as a new professor, I was asked by my students to define a simple, commonly used word: entrepreneurship.

It was odd that neither I nor my colleagues had a decent definition of the word. The dictionaries and textbooks weren't much help either, providing meanings that were non-specific or too limiting even when they sounded plausible. If it seems easy, go ahead and attempt to define words like *entrepreneurship* and *innovation* in a way that's concise and specific, without being so general as to cover lots of other activities. Even the leading entrepreneurship program where I've taught, Babson College, promotes itself as a school for entrepreneurs of all kinds. That's brilliant marketing, but not so helpful when it comes to figuring out what an entrepreneur is or does. In an effort to prevent a mutiny by my bright and assertive students who challenged me on this point during my first day of teaching, I started to pay attention to how words are defined.

To help us along I'll offer definitions for: **success, succeeding, failure, failing, value** and **resource**. These are my own definitions and hopefully I've done them justice. Having common definitions for these key terms will allow us to launch into an intelligent conversation about Smart Experiments, the value of achieving and succeeding more, and more consistently, over the long run, and how to do all of our experiments well.

Let's start by defining success. It's no big surprise that success means different things to different people. In fact, most of us think about success in personal and specific terms. "I'll be a success as soon as I achieve X." The same is true for failure, such as when something goes wrong and we say (to ourselves) "I'm such an idiot because I couldn't make Y happen," even when the odds were clearly stacked against us. For purposes of our discussion, we need definitions of these words that are broader and more concrete. So here goes:

> **Success** is having what we want or wanting what we have, preferably both. Conversely, **failure** means not having what we want and not wanting what we have. Saying that someone is "a success" or "a failure" is a judgment made by one person about another person (and the two of them may not necessarily agree). Success and failure are subjective judgments that we make at specific moments in time. They're snapshots of the past or present that don't foretell the future. Someone labeled as a failure today may be a success tomorrow.

> **Succeeding** is different from *success* because it's the process of accumulating value. It's a story that unfolds, with future chapters to be written. A person can be at a low-point in life and speedily accumulating value (a temporary failure in the ongoing process of succeeding and becoming a success). Or a person can be at the top of his game and in the process of losing it all (a temporary success in the life of someone who's in the process of failing). As such, **failing** is the process of losing value. Succeeding and failing represent movement in a particular direction, irrespective of one's present situation.

Would you rather be a success or succeeding? What if we start to envision the process of accumulating value as desirable—as success itself?

Succeeding and failing are processes that happen over time. The scale at which we perceive a process changes our perspective. For example, we could be hiking up a mountain and come to a big gaping valley in front of us. The long view, however, is to see the mountaintop. In terms of succeeding and failing, we might be failing miserably over the course of hours or days, and succeeding amazingly over a longer period of months or years. Sustainable success requires us to take the long view—to see the things in our daily lives as part of a larger whole, an extended effort. When we adopt this big picture view, we find that we're less fazed by the outcomes that may not suit us (and that get labeled as failures), and more humbled by success. The present is just the start of a wide open future that's ours to create.

IT IS WISE TO KEEP IN MIND
THAT NEITHER SUCCESS NOR
FAILURE IS EVER FINAL.

Roger Babson

Since succeeding is the process of accumulating value, and failing is the process of losing value, let's discuss the concept of **value**. While we can say that we value something or someone, I'll use the word as a noun with this definition:

Value is any specific benefit or utility provided by a resource.

Let me offer an example. My bike is a resource that's a collection of tangible, intangible and monetary value. Physically it lets me move from place to place quickly and efficiently; psychologically it keeps me happy as the fresh air rushes past my face and the pedaling makes me feel like I'm getting a workout; and it saves me gas money, too. I can even trade it for something else of value. Like my bike, every resource represents a collection of three kinds of value:

1) Tangible value arises from the physical features or actions of a resource

2) Intangible value is anything that informs or motivates a person's actions

3) Monetary value is a resource's capacity to be traded for something else

Resources are organized and recognizable collections of value.

Even resources that seem to possess only one kind of value are combinations of all three. Consider a dollar bill or any paper currency. Most people would say that it's money, which it is, and that it represents monetary value, which it does! It's also tangible and has several possible physical uses. For example, I can make a paper airplane out of a dollar bill, which has nothing to do with its monetary value. Likewise, money has intangible (emotional) value. Throughout history it has elicited the best and worst in people. The general point is that every resource is a combination of these three kinds of value.

EVERY RESOURCE IS A COLLECTION
OF THREE KINDS OF VALUE

Value is everywhere. Everything we see, touch, hold, listen to, know and feel in our hearts has value. The key is to see, in this amazing universe of resources, the value that is most useful to us and to others.

In order not to be overwhelmed, let's start with the big resources that we have in our lives. Think about what each of these resources offers to us in terms of tangible value, intangible value and monetary value:

- Health and energy—our ability to use our bodies to make things happen—is our greatest resource. The highest achievers know this (more often than not) and do what it takes to be physically and mentally energized.

- If each of us is his or her own best resource, then other people are next on the list. The relationships we have with family, friends and colleagues offer us the ability to extend our capabilities to get more done.

- Physical objects can be extremely helpful as well, and they come in many shapes and sizes. These are the assets, tools, materials and physical 'things' that we leverage to be more productive and effective in our lives.

- Money is the wild card that can help compensate for our lack of other types of resources. View money as a way to store value—a resource that we can unlock by trading the money for what we need in the future.

Seeing the value that's all around us means knowing the resources we possess and can invest in our experiments. This lets us do the best Smart Experiments.

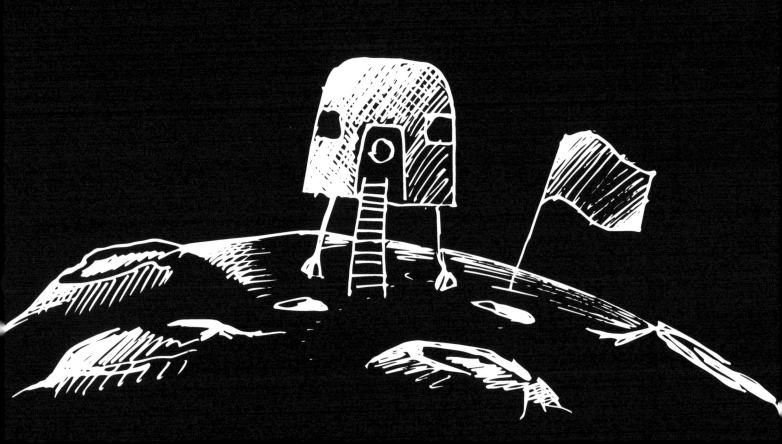

SMART EXPERIMENTS

ALL LIFE IS AN EXPERIMENT.

Ralph Waldo Emerson

 Virtually everything we do is an experiment that tests our abilities and allows us to explore the world around us. From the smallest courtesy extended to a friend, to the most complex global initiative, we experiment by investing our available resources to discover what will happen next.

Experiments provoke the world to answer questions, even when we may not be asking them. What happens when I do this? Can we make that? What if we don't meet them? Or we pursue something differently? Experiments empower us to discover a path, or oftentimes simply stumble, into an unpredictable future. They help us to learn about ourselves, other people and the world around us.

The computer scientist Alan Kay is credited with saying that "the best way to predict the future is to invent it." Experiments invite us to take a first step, test the boundaries of our reality, acquire new resources (composed of tangible, intangible and monetary value), and invent a future for ourselves by taking one step after another.

★

THE BEST WAY TO PREDICT THE FUTURE IS TO INVENT IT.

A detail that Emerson's beautiful quote anticipates, but doesn't say outright, is that there are good experiments and there are bad experiments. I don't mean good and bad outcomes (both succeeding and failing will happen), but rather that there are both smart ways of going about doing experiments, and not-so-smart ways of doing them. Doing Smart Experiments that tilt the odds of accumulating value in our favor is critical to succeeding over the long run.

To illustrate this, let's look at an obviously bad experiment. Imagine testing the hardness of a brick wall by running full-speed into it. Doing this, of course, would not be a Smart Experiment. While intentionally running into a wall is an extreme example of a bad experiment, it makes the simple but critical point that some experiments are destined to lead to worse outcomes than others.

Bad experiments happen for a variety of reasons. While they may result from a flawed process, such as acting without thinking, most often they happen for much more subtle reasons. Commonly, they lack meaning and are inconsistent with our priorities, generate low-value payouts even when they go well, and anticipate potential problems that we aren't prepared to either see or resolve. Poor execution also happens, often when value is left uncollected at the end of an experiment—meaning that at times we don't finish what we start. Clearly there are several simple things we can do to make our experiments better.

Smart Experiments involve a process having four steps that work together to place us on a higher trajectory. Although Smart Experiments don't guarantee positive outcomes every time, doing Smart Experiments has a big cumulative effect over time. This effect is similar to compound interest. It's a simple yet powerful concept—the difference between placing a series of bets with better odds vs. worse odds. Why wouldn't everyone want to go with the best possible odds and always do experiments with a higher probability of succeeding? Sure, we'll win some and we'll lose some, but the point is to win more over the long run. The better we do things, the higher our trajectory takes us over time. Now that we see why doing Smart Experiments make so much sense, let's examine the process step by step and, in the next chapter, hear a few stories.

CHOOSE YOUR TRAJECTORY

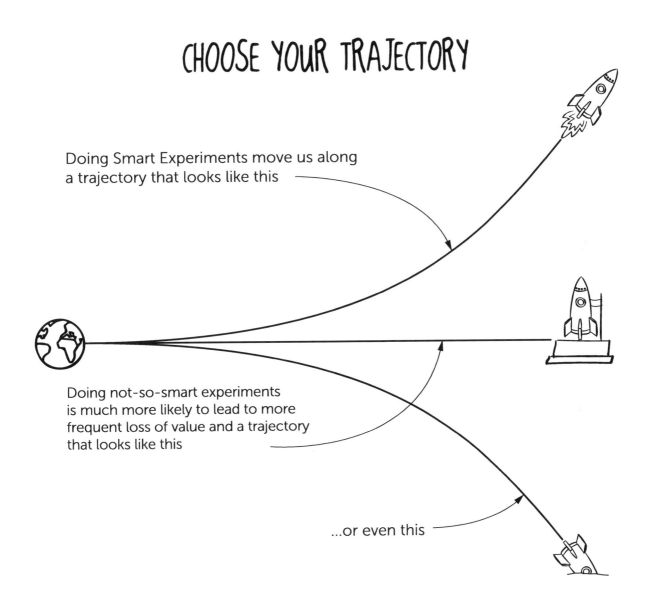

Doing Smart Experiments move us along
a trajectory that looks like this

Doing not-so-smart experiments
is much more likely to lead to more
frequent loss of value and a trajectory
that looks like this

...or even this

THE SMART EXPERIMENT

Every Smart Experiment is made up of four steps. These are shown in the overview diagram at right. Performing each of the four steps enables us to do experiments that are meaningful and likely to lead us to optimal outcomes. The goal of every Smart Experiment is to acquire new resources so that we can do ever bigger and better experiments. Smart Experiments propel us into a future that's sometimes surprising and most always rewarding.

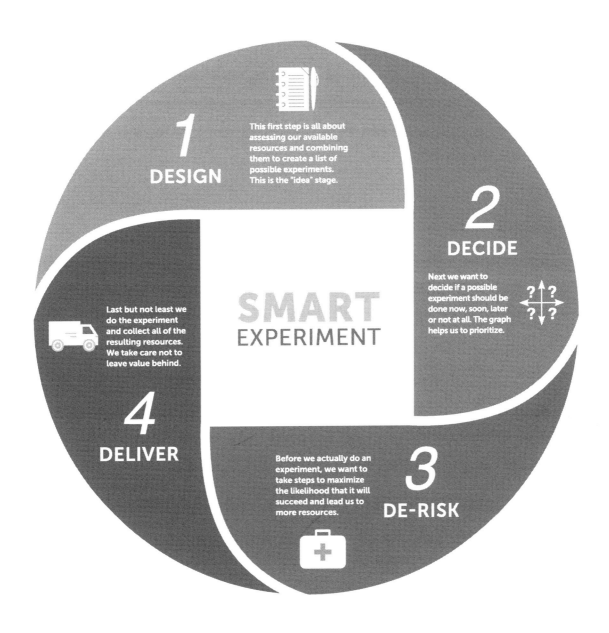

1 DESIGN

This first step is all about assessing our available resources and combining them to create a list of possible experiments. This is the "idea" stage.

2 DECIDE

Next we want to decide if a possible experiment should be done now, soon, later or not at all. The graph helps us to prioritize.

SMART EXPERIMENT

Last but not least we do the experiment and collect all of the resulting resources. We take care not to leave value behind.

4 DELIVER

Before we actually do an experiment, we want to take steps to maximize the likelihood that it will succeed and lead us to more resources.

3 DE-RISK

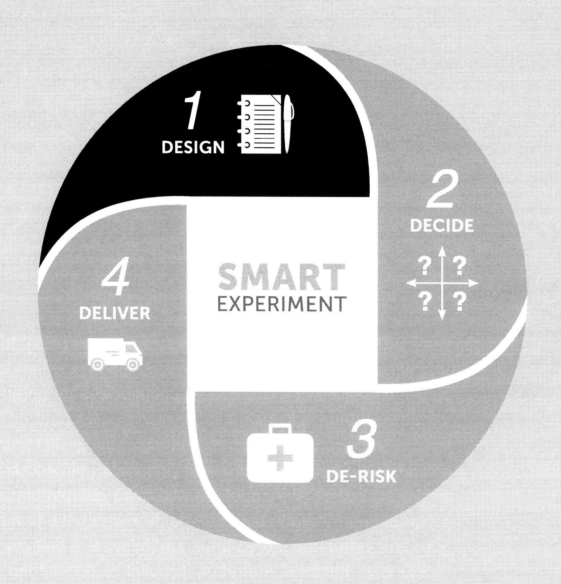

STEP 1: **DESIGN**

Every Smart Experiment starts with Design. This involves assessing the resources under our control, thinking about ways to combine their value, and coming up with an intention, plan, proposal, etc. Whatever we decide to call it, this is the thing that we'll evaluate and prioritize (in step 2) in order to determine if we'll prepare (in step 3) to do the experiment (in step 4). If not, we'll stick with **Design** and continue to brainstorm more possibilities.

Like the other steps in a Smart Experiment, **Design** may be done in a variety of ways, depending on our unique circumstances. At times we'll want to design an experiment quickly, such as when we have resources that we want to deploy rapidly. At other times, **Design** may involve a more formal process that takes months or even years. This is often the case for complex or costly projects, especially those that are difficult to revise once started. Another variable is whether an experiment is being designed by an individual or a team. No matter what the case, the objective is the same: to generate ideas.

★

IN DESIGN, WE GENERATE IDEAS FOR EXPERIMENTS THAT WE THINK WE MAY WANT TO DO.

In **Design**, we generate ideas for experiments that we think we may want to do. In Step 1, it's our time to brainstorm. This isn't the time to decide or prioritize, nor is it the time to do any experiments. This comes later. Our goal is to create a list of possible experiments that we can give further thought to. Some of these will be pursued soon; others will percolate in our minds until they are ready to be moved forward. For now, we want to generate as many ideas as we can without prejudging them. Even our craziest ideas can be useful.

It's most helpful to break the Design step into two parts: assess the resources we have, and then combine our resources to design possible experiments.

A) ASSESS THE RESOURCES WE HAVE

Before we design a Smart Experiment, we need to know what resources we have available to invest. One of the common mistakes that many of us make is to dream up experiments that cannot be done because we lack the resources to actually do them. It's only possible to invest value that we control.

A great way to assess value we have is to develop an inventory of resources. Written lists are helpful, especially when working as a team. Writing down a list of resources helps us to document and remember them, which is important for the next part of the process. With experience, however, individuals often keep things in their minds. I find that having an intuitive sense of what value is helps a lot, and creating written inventories of our resources lets us visualize all of the tangible, intangible and monetary value that we have available to invest.

Whether written or in memory, it's great to keep track of:

- tangible value such as physical assets we own or control

- intangible value like information, knowledge, our emotions

- intangible value such as our skills and abilities to make things

- people we know and value they have, e.g., know-how, abilities

- financial value like available cash and credit, access to investors

B) COMBINE RESOURCES TO DESIGN POSSIBLE EXPERIMENTS

Once we have an inventory of all of the resources available for us to invest (even though we'll only invest portions of their value for any given experiment), it's time to dream up possible experiments for evaluation in Step 2.

We do this by creating unique combinations of value. For example, what would happen if we put Person X into Laboratory Y with Equipment Z?

As a simple demonstration—if only to prove a point—I often suggest randomly selecting three different items from an inventory. What experiment can we do with them? More often than not, we can design a possible experiment.

Of course some possible experiments will come to us with ease. For example, we may know an expert who can help us, in combination with knowledge and a prototype that we have available, to make a sale to a prospective new client. That's a great combination of value and a design for a possible experiment that we'll want to consider for Step 2 in our Smart Experiment process.

Coming up with designs for possible experiments isn't always easy or obvious. This is where creativity comes into play, and why it's such a valuable skill for all of us to develop. The fundamental goal of creativity in the **Design** step is to see synergistic combinations of value that can be invested together. Oftentimes the least obvious combinations lead to our most intriguing experiments.

When it comes to keeping up a flow of designs for experiments, I also suggest always being on the lookout for new resources, and imagining the possibilities of combining this new value with value that we already have. This makes **Design** an ongoing process that leads to a consistent flow of possible experiments.

STEP 1: DESIGN

What value do I possess?

tangible	Intangible	Monetary
_____	_____	_____
_____	_____	_____
_____	_____	_____
_____	_____	_____

What experiments might I do?

_____

_____

_____

_____

A. Ganss

Over the years I've noticed that people who become confident at assessing resources and creating experiments in the Design step can get sloppy. It's simple human nature to start prejudging and advancing (or eliminating) ideas for experiments prematurely.

It helps to stay open-minded. Many of the best experiments are easily dismissed in the Design step—before they can be modified in light of new value that we later acquire. What's currently infeasible may soon become possible.

At the opposite end of the spectrum, many people prematurely advance ideas from the Design step—straight past steps 2 and 3—to Delivery of the experiment in step 4. This is impulsive and definitely not a Smart Experiment. As we will see, steps 2 and 3 are essential to the process and should never be skipped over.

The lesson here is that sustainable success requires us to achieve and maintain a sense of humility. On the one hand, it's great to be confident about our ability to assess resources and design lots of possible experiments. On the other hand, too much confidence coming up with "brilliant ideas" can lead us to conclude that a designed experiment should be done right away, or not at all. We need to avoid this trap. In fact, all four of the steps in a Smart Experiment matter.

★

ALL FOUR STEPS IN A SMART EXPERIMENT MATTER.

Stay humble and keep in mind that Smart Experiments are smart for several reasons. As we learn about all four of the steps in a Smart Experiment, consider the role each plays in the process, and the benefits of doing all of them well.

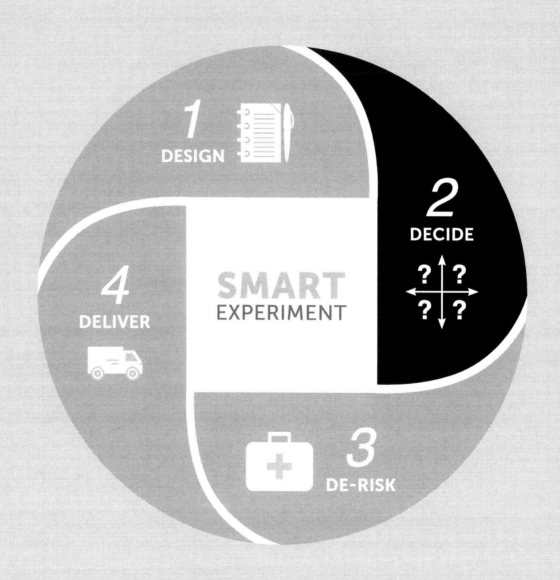

STEP 2: **DECIDE**

 Our brains want us to act on our ideas. In general, they want us to believe that all of our ideas are brilliant and, from that moment on, all we want to do is to justify our brilliance by leaping into action. At other times, we discuss a prospective experiment with friends or colleagues. This is a lose-lose situation because when people we respect tell us how extraordinary our idea is we feel stuck having to prove them right, and when they criticize us we feel the need to prove them wrong! For whatever reason, we often jump straight from an idea for a possible experiment to doing the experiment, without a lot of thought about whether or not it's worth doing the experiment in the first place. This is where **Decide** comes into play.

The **Decide** step keeps us focused on the experiments that matter most, based on our personal (and organizational) goals. So it pays to know who we are and what we value. The highest performers spend a lot of time thinking about this, and re-evaluate personal and organizational missions often. We should always want to pursue the things that are most meaningful to us, and stay away from the endless possible distractions that keep us from our true purpose.

The **Decide** step helps in two ways. First, if we're thinking about doing a single experiment, it suggests whether we should do it now, take some further action (delay or share), or not do it at all. Also, if we're considering multiple possible experiments, the Decide step helps us to evaluate possible experiments relative to one another in order to learn our priorities. Decide helps us know what to do when—an essential skill if we want to achieve and succeed more.

To decide if we'll move forward with an experiment (and take it to Step 3 in the Smart Experiment process), we need to consider two things. *First*, we need to determine whether a possible experiment is worth doing. *Second*, we want to know if the experiment that we're contemplating is more (or less) important than other possible experiments.

The first decision is critical because we always want to be doing things that matter most and that are meaningful to us (and our organizations) and to avoid doing experiments that aren't likely to have meaning or create value. Too many people get caught up doing things that aren't meaningful or valuable to them. They've never given much thought to what matters most to them, which can lead to a life that lacks purpose. Knowing our priorities is critical because none of us have the time or other resources to do it all. We have limited resources to invest at any point in time. The **Decide** step tells us which of our experiments to do now, consider for later, pursue with a partner, or not do at all.

While there are several ways to approach the **Decide** step, I like the power and simplicity of an approach that balances the expected value of an experiment (its meaningfulness, in essence) with the potential loss of invested value—its risk profile. Plotting these together helps us to see and settle on our priorities.

The graph on the following page may look simple, and at the conceptual level it is. However it's often not easy to plot our experiments onto it. This turns out to be more art than science. As you can see, the horizontal (x) axis represents the expected value to be derived from a given experiment, and the vertical (y) axis represents the potential for loss. We use this model because it works well as a tool to help us compare and prioritize all kinds of possible experiments.

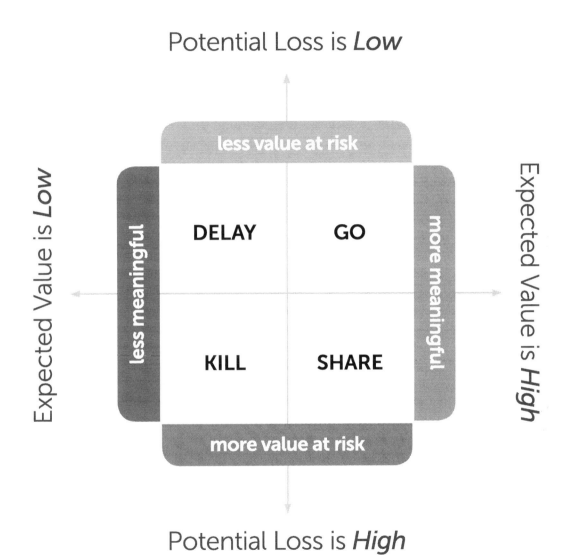

The decision graph helps us prioritize our experiments.

Expected value can be determined in a variety of ways, from the simple to the sophisticated. One simple approach is to ask the question, "If we do the experiment, is it likely to be meaningful? In other words, is the anticipated payoff high enough to be useful? If we invest resources to do the experiment, what value are we likely to receive in return? In order to plot this, we can use objective value (like dollars) or subjective value (like rating 'payoff' from 1 to 10) or a combination of these. It can get complicated quickly.

A simple subjective approach can be quite effective in plotting our experiment along the horizontal axis. Experiments with trivial (or even negative) payoffs go to the left of those with more valuable (positive) payoffs. Just compare one experiment to another, and rank them, placing them to the left or right of one another. Other techniques can be used, including well-known financial analyses, such as a calculation of the expected net present value (eNPV) of an experiment. The key is to appreciate that the higher the expected value of a possible experiment, the farther to the right it gets plotted on our decision graph and the more desirable it's likely to be for us to pursue it.

Potential loss is represented on the vertical axis. Potential loss means the quantity (and not the probability) of invested value that we could lose if things go badly during execution of the experiment. By "badly," I mean that we lose as much value as possible as a result of having done the experiment. For example, if we invest $5.00, a bag of supplies, and our ego into an experiment and it's a complete flop, then we've lost $5.00, used up our supplies and also bruised our ego. That's a big loss to some people, especially the bruised ego! So the vertical axis represents "the most we have to lose," with experiments that could result in higher losses being plotted lower down.

I'm not oblivious to the fact that it's challenging to quantify certain forms of value, such as a bruised ego. In practice, most of us intuitively know whether a payoff (in terms of total value of all kinds) for an experiment is higher or lower than for some other experiment, and the same holds true for the idea of potential loss. My research shows that the highest achievers are decisive and also wrong a significant portion of the time. This doesn't seem to make a difference because, quite simply, their decisiveness leads them to do more Smart Experiments and the results compound over time. On the other hand, big companies often use sophisticated techniques to determine the potential loss, such as calculating exchange rates for different kinds of value that enable the creation of a single quantitative metric. The key is to come up with a system that works in practice.

RESEARCH SHOWS THAT THE HIGHEST ACHIEVERS ARE DECISIVE AND ALSO WRONG A SIGNIFICANT PORTION OF THE TIME.

As soon as we figure out an expected value and potential loss for a particular experiment, we can plot it on the graph and see which quadrant it ends up in. Where an experiment gets plotted on the graph tells us a lot about it:

GO When an experiment lands in the upper right quadrant of our graph it means that the experiment has a high expected value and low potential loss. Wonderful! This is an experiment we want to do. The higher up and to the right, the better.

SHARE Experiments that land in the lower right quadrant may be worthy, but we can't afford their potential loss (at least at the moment), which could be a drain on our resources or possibly ruin us. In these instances, we need to share (partner or offload) some of the potential loss to somebody else. Usually this means that we will also need to share the benefits, but if we want to do the experiment enough this is the compromise we may need to make by engaging with a partner to accept some of the risk.

DELAY When an experiment finds its home in the upper left quadrant, this means that we should hold off. The payoff just isn't big enough (at least at the moment) compared with other possible experiments. If we have nothing better to do, such as having no ideas that live in the upper right quadrant, then maybe we'll think more about it. In general, experiments in the upper left quadrant have the potential to be big distractions.

KILL The lower left quadrant is the prison that holds all of our bad ideas, meaning those experimental designs that have a low expected value (not meaningful) and a high probable loss (greatest potential to keep us from being able to go forward). We'll keep track of these and keep them in our sights, but we shouldn't do them. They're dangerous for the time being.

ACTION EXPRESSES PRIORITIES.

Mahatma Gandhi

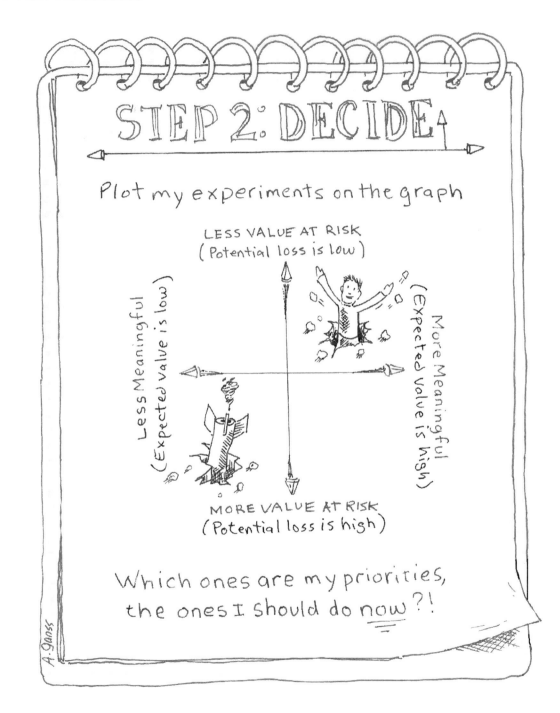

DECIDING WHAT TO DO NEXT

The bottom line of **Decide** is to focus on the experiments in the Go quadrant first. These are our priorities, our best ideas, even though some will be better to do than others. Do the experiments that are plotted the farthest up and to the right—these are our highest priority experiments.

Once we move beyond these experiments we can consider those in the lower right quadrant, the Share experiments. These require partners to help us limit our potential loss. In exchange for accepting some of the potential loss of value (even if it never happens), partners will most likely expect to share in the upside. That's fair and we'll partner in a way that works for everyone.

Sometimes we may want to visit the Delay quadrant, but generally only after we've done all of our higher expected value experiments (those to the right). Delay experiments don't have the best payoffs relative to our mission, but they may be worth doing, especially when we can find ways to improve upon them. Interestingly, these experiments often have surprising outcomes. One trick is to find ways to make them worthwhile by combining them with new resources.

Don't entirely neglect ideas in the Kill quadrant. Periodically revisit them to see if any can be recategorized. Has anything changed in light of new resources we've accumulated? For example, do we now have new skills or partnerships that improve the expected value and lower the potential loss to make any of these ideas feasible? It's worth periodically reevaluating these experiments.

It's worth revisiting old ideas for experiments every so often, too. Even when we don't pursue a particular design, old ideas are a great source of new ones. They provide inspiration and a sense of how we're evolving over time.

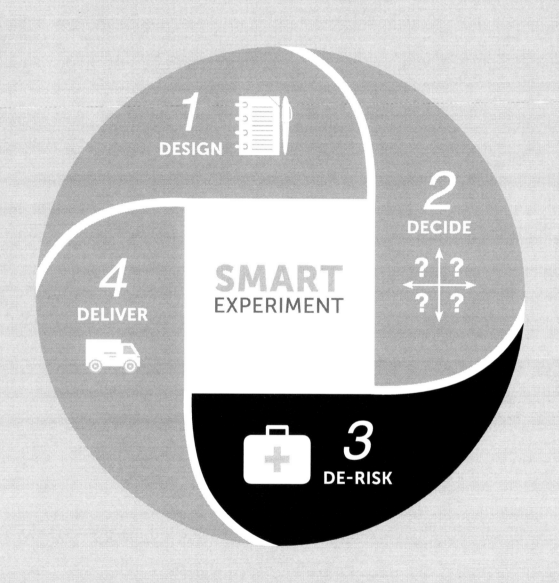

STEP 3: **DE-RISK**

 In a commencement address at Williams College in 2012, surgeon and author Atul Gawande talked about an article that appeared in the *New England Journal of Medicine* three years earlier. The article noted that inpatient surgical death rates at some hospitals are nearly double what they are at other hospitals. Why is this the case? Is it true that hospitals with better outcomes have better surgeons? That's what most people think.

In fact, the research concluded that it wasn't any difference in the quality of the surgeons, or even differences in the complication rates, which were nearly the same for the best and worst hospitals. In fact, the top hospitals did a better job of dealing with the *inevitable* complications of surgery—by reacting quickly to make things right as soon as possible. The best hospitals don't fail less; they rescue more. Dr. Gawande concluded his speech with these words:

> *You will take risks, and you will have failures. But it's what happens [during an experiment] that is defining. A failure often does not have to be a failure at all. However, you have to be ready for it—will you admit when things go wrong? Will you take steps to set them right?—because the difference between triumph and defeat, you'll find, isn't about willingness to take the risk in the first place. It's about mastery of rescue."*

Mastery of rescue. What a beautiful phrase to convey that we must prepare for the inevitable if we wish to see more triumphs in our lives! Sustained success depends on being able to find and fix problems as soon as they arise.

WHAT'S WRONG? FIX IT NOW.

The third step in every Smart Experiment is to De-Risk it. This involves a series of actions. First, we identify the biggest potential Hotspots (also known as our potential problems, hurdles, challenges, weaknesses, etc.) for our experiment. Next, our job is to figure out how we will prepare in order to rapidly recognize and respond to each of these Hotspots. Last but not least, during delivery of our experiment, we address any and all Hotspots. Since most problems get bigger over time, being able to rapidly recognize and respond to Hotspots has major implications for achievement and success.

A) IDENTIFY THE BIGGEST HOTSPOTS

Most of the time this is straightforward. Suppose we want to take a few friends for a hike through a forest that we've never explored before. What are the most likely Hotspots? What are the big things that could adversely affect the group? Here's my list: being out of shape, becoming dehydrated, getting lost or injured. Every experiment has its Hotspots. Think them through and make a list.

B) PREPARE TO RECOGNIZE AND RESPOND TO THEM

It's imperative that each Hotspot needs a rapid recognition and response plan associated with it. Rapid recognition can be done in a variety of ways, from the simple (like training people to look for signs that something is about to go wrong), to the complex (making use of sensors and technology, for example). Each Hotspot compels us to think about the best way to quickly see it and respond to it. The best ways to prepare typically involve things like training and knowledge and experience, including simulations and practice.

For our hike in the forest, preparations will include being sure that everyone is in shape, knows how to prevent (and recognize the signs/symptoms of) dehydration, understands our route and basic navigation (and has the proper tools). At least one member of the group will also be trained in wilderness first aid.

Now we are ready to rapidly recognize and respond

In our best experiments, when we have thought about Hotspots and prepared for them, the result is either a *non-response* or an *automatic response*. A *non-response* is the one we never have to implement because our preparation served us well. For example, getting everyone in shape before our hike lowers the chances that anyone gets physically exhausted to a point that it becomes an issue. An *automatic response* is one we barely need to think about. We kick into action to make things right. This happens with extensive training, knowledge, simulation, and other forms of preparedness. If one of the hikers cuts her leg, an *automatic response* stops the bleeding and then efficiently cleans and dresses the wound. This allows the group to keep progressing with minimal loss, worry, distraction and future danger.

What about the times when something goes wrong that we haven't prepared for? This happens, and there are many examples of problems that we just can't predict or that are such long-shots that they (quite reasonably) may not have been worth thinking about. A meteorite perchance? By preparing for as many eventualities as practically possible we prepare for the unexpected. It's the best we can do.

When it comes to de-risking a Smart Experiment, a little thought goes a long way. Identify Hotspots and prepare to rapidly recognize and respond to them. This allows us to deal with issues when they're smaller and more readily resolved. So before we do any experiment, **De-Risk** it as much as possible.

BY FAILING TO PREPARE,
YOU ARE PREPARING TO FAIL.

Benjamin Franklin

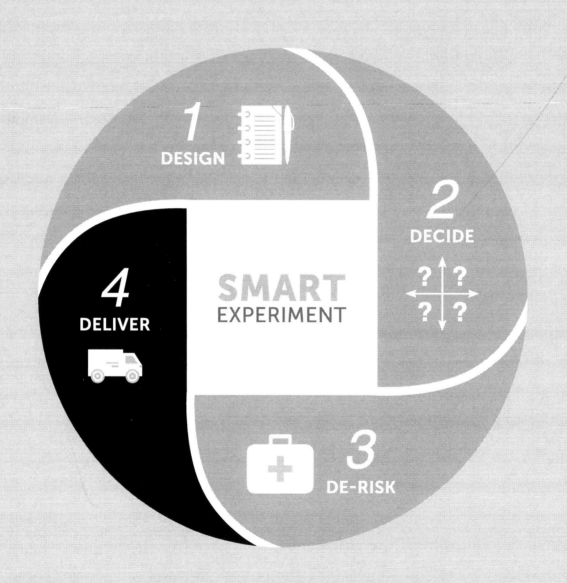

STEP 4: **DELIVER**

It's now (finally!) time to Deliver the experiment. To **Deliver** an experiment involves two things. First, we invest the resources that we've committed and execute our plan of action. We do the experiment. Second, we harvest (collect) the value that results from our experiment.

The proper execution of an experiment is a topic on which there's a lot to say, so I'll stick to the most important points. My research shows that most of us can do the Smart Experiments we design in Step 1 successfully, if we've followed Steps 1, 2 and 3. In other words, the execution of Smart Experiments isn't generally an issue for most people or even big organizations. If we have the resources we need and follow the first three steps of a Smart Experiment as presented, then "running" our experiment is actually the easy part. This is the case most of the time.

The second part of **Deliver** is where many of us get caught up: harvesting all of the value that arises from an experiment. I place special emphasis on this point because I've learned that not only do the highest achievers harvest value especially well, it's something that others don't do well—despite being a key step (and upon reflection an obvious one) for the accumulation of value.

Here's what I mean by harvesting all of the value from an experiment: When things go well (that is, when we're pleased with the outcome) we shouldn't just walk away with the most valuable aspects of the outcome. Every new resource has potential value and it makes a lot of sense to make the effort to collect all available value, and not just skim the cream. On the other hand...

When things don't go well, we shouldn't run away! It's too easy to want to distance ourselves from those experiments that don't go as we hoped, but this is exactly the wrong response. By doing this, we miss a massive opportunity to learn and grow. In fact, experiments that don't go well offer the greatest opportunities to acquire new knowledge, relationships and just about every other kind of value. So how can we be sure that we're harvesting all the value at the end of an experiment?

Begin by **speaking with everyone involved.** Following every Smart Experiment, we want to discover what went well, and what didn't. An objective is to collect data and grasp knowledge that resulted from our investment of resources. This will involve actions like talking, observing, exploring, probing and more.

Then, **pick up the pieces.** Experiments spin off many disparate pieces of value that we'll want to gather up. We want to glean all the tangible, intangible and monetary value that's produced at the conclusion of every experiment. And we shouldn't underestimate the value that some seemingly insignificant bit might contribute in the future. These are often the most intriguing resources.

Finally, **clean up any mess.** This is easy to skip over, but avoiding the clean-up would be a big mistake. If anything went wrong, we should do our best to make things right. Morals and ethics aside, this is a chance to enhance our reputation, an important intangible value. A little tidying up can lead to big surprises.

To **Deliver** is to do experiments to the best of our abilities, including harvesting all of the value that results. Remember that, at the end of the day, experiments are investments of resources, and succeeding *means* accumulating new value. We can only accumulate new value if we follow through and gather it all up.

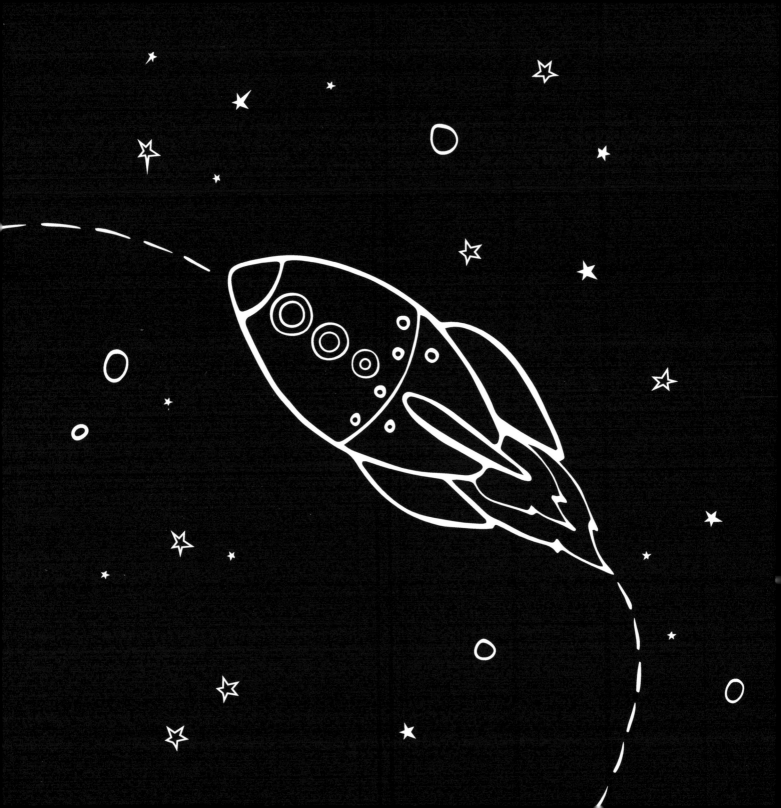

REAL-LIFE EXAMPLES

REAL-LIFE EXAMPLES

All of us can succeed more through the power of **Smart Experiments**, Relationships and Expertise—the three building blocks of sustainable success. Now that we know *how to do* Smart Experiments, I'll share the stories of four people whose lives are full of experiments and experiences. My purpose isn't to place anyone on a pedestal; instead I offer examples. Four uniquely accomplished people describe, in their own words, how experiments have shaped their extraordinary lives.

PETER RALSTON

His Experiment: Creating Lasting Images

Peter Ralston is the first to say he's led a 'Forest Gump' life. After growing up in the idyllic countryside of Chadds Ford, Pennsylvania, he soon found himself immersed in the adventurous life of a globe-trotting photographer. Then he was introduced to the coast of Maine. He fell in love with its people and places, and most notably its islands. In 1983, Peter cofounded the Island Institute with Philip Conkling, which is now a 50-person organization that's dedicated to supporting and maintaining the year-round communities on Maine's islands. Throughout his three decades at the institute, Peter chronicled island life and published the *Island Journal*, where many of his iconic photographs have appeared. In 2003, Colby College awarded Peter an honorary Doctor of Laws degree for his work. Today Peter owns the Ralston Gallery in Rockport, Maine, where he shares the people and places he loves through his stories and photographs.

Peter always seems to be pondering "What happens if I...?" and then he quickly leaps into action. He calls himself a walking experiment and all of his decisions come from a place of passion. From the wild adventurous days of his youth, to his present-day status as one of the nation's most prized photographers, his experiments are part of his regular routine. Through these experiences, and by embracing life's many surprises, he's invented an extraordinary life.

grew up in a house in Chadds Ford, Pennsylvania. *My grandparents, proper types on both sides, were horrified when my parents bought this house way out in the country. And it was the greatest thing! This funky, old, rundown, beautiful, grey, stone Quaker-built house, which was part of an old mill property. And the next year, Andy and Betsy Wyeth* bought the other half of the property, including the mill and the granary, right down to the floodplain.*

I had this idyllic childhood—the river, the woods up behind us. I had a little boat, a great canoe, and my dog. I was always exploring. We also had a creative and nurturing mother who gave her life to us. And next door I've got this Chernobyl, this nuclear energy with Andy and Betsy who were second parents to me.

Then I was shipped off to private school. At age 15, I ended up in France as a Youth Ambassador, some program where I had to wear a little blue blazer. Well, it turned into a joke because two other guys and I broke away from the group to the consternation of the adults. We had better things to do. All my hormones, not to mention my high energy and ADD, it was off the charts. When I returned to school I didn't do well. I got thrown out a week before the end of my junior year and sent back home to public school. Having been to Paris I thought I was worldly so I quit high school. I mean, I just said enough of this.

All this time I knew that I wanted to be a photographer. I had said this to my parents. I wanted to go to college and study photography and the arts. But now we're well into 1960's and everybody's coming apart. Kids are doing really crazy stuff. The world's going out and protesting. We were being environmental,

*Andrew Wyeth (1917-2009) was an internationally acclaimed artist and one of the foremost American painters of the 20th Century. His works centered on his homes in Chadds Ford, Pennsylvania and Maine. One of his paintings, *Christina's World*, is among the best-known works of the 20th Century. Betsy, his wife, was a major influence on his life.

thinking about stuff. But it was really about youthful rebellion and throwing it back in our parents' faces.

I headed off into the world with no money, with a mediocre camera, and I was going to be a photographer. I had a few jobs like driving a farm truck and doing technical writing, but always with a camera at my side. And then I gradually figured out how to make something of it. At the time publishing was centered in New York. I'd go to magazines and show them my slides of sensitive shots of the valley. I realized that I could make nice pictures. That's what it was back then. I could make decent photographs, and people would pay me for them.

Everything came through experimentation with my camera and selling my work. My initials aren't 'PR' for nothing. Did you know I only studied photography two times? For my 21st birthday my grandmother gave me a workshop with Ansel Adams in Yosemite. That was so cool. Then a seminal moment came with this guy at the Maine Photographic Workshops, my one other formal course. He introduced me to somebody at Life magazine. So I dutifully show up in New York and I have four or five pages of slides that I showed him. And they're pictures of spider webs in the morning dew. I wince when I think about what I shared that day. I received a great gift from him. He scolded me, "Never ever present yourself to anybody like this again. You're showing me a hundred pictures and you should have brought one sheet, and you edit it down and you only show your best and don't try to overwhelm." But he saw something, I guess, and he said, "You know, some of this is pretty good. There's something here." And I get the name

> **EVERYTHING CAME THROUGH EXPERIMENTATION WITH MY CAMERA AND SELLING MY WORK.**

> **I WAS A F***ING WALKING EXPERIMENT... I WAS A PETRI DISH, AND GOD KNOWS WHAT WAS GROWING BUT IT WAS GROWING.**

for the Art Director at The Today Show. So I go over there and she loves my stuff and puts it on this national morning show. So I lucked out because I showed up, did the experiment, and left with a heck of a lot more than I started with. Every morning millions of people see my work. I'm feeling I'm hot shit. But, at the same time I also felt humble. I didn't know what I was doing. But this opening let me pitch to more magazines. I talked my way into them and got some pretty good gigs.

I was a f***ing walking experiment at the time. I was a petri dish, and God knows what was growing but it was growing. Really. So I just kept on going in this direction with a camera always with me. One day I realized that there were stories out there. This really opened up the world around me. It got to the point where I actually got paid to travel to super cool places to take the pictures that told the stories.

After the insanity of New York, I decided to head back to the garden, to Chadds Ford, and settled down a bit. I started getting much closer, and on a much more intimate sort of adult level, with Andy and Betsy. That's when the education started. That's when my real work with them began, when they started taking me to shows, giving me books, nurturing me, guiding me. I didn't realize it at the time how deliberate and comprehensive and generous they were being. I mean, it was just amazing when I think about it. And I was clueless to some of this. I choke up when I think how loving and persistent they were with me. They later said, "We saw something in you." You know, how can you ever say thank you enough or live up to that kind of faith and encouragement?

In '78, I was at a dinner at Andy and Betsy's house in Chadds Ford. Betsy had this way about her, she could be very direct. She leans across the dinner table and points her finger at me and says, 'You are coming to Maine this summer.' It wasn't so much an invitation; it was an edict.

Earlier in my childhood, when Andy and Betsy came back from Maine I would run down to see them. These paintings of Maine would come back with them and it was the most exotic stuff. They would tell me these fantastic stories about who these people were or what these places were. So it became clear that they waited until just the right moment to make their move with me. It was like I was the next painting in a way. Like they could envision things. Talk about experiments. They did them. I was one of theirs.

> ## ALL OF MY CRAZY EXPERIMENTS HAD SYNERGISTICALLY BROUGHT ME TO THIS MOMENT.

Maine was this very different place, but as soon as I arrived I knew that I was put on earth to be here. My first summer in Maine was six weeks. The next summer was eight weeks. I really knew this was it. I didn't know what exactly the path was going to be for me in this new life, but I knew Maine was where it would happen.

Betsy bought an island and put me in charge of figuring out what to do with it. I was her right hand guy. She asked me to talk to Philip Conklin, a naturalist. He comes out and we trumped around. Philip and I liked each other right off the bat. Fast-forward and we started seeing other islands, because now I'm in Maine. And so here I was fresh, smitten, absolutely more than in love. I mean, I was just swept away by what I was seeing here. This was my new garden. All of my crazy experiments had synergistically brought me to this moment, this place in time.

Philip and I started the Island Institute in '83. It's original purpose was to offer forestry and conservation services. That soon grew into a vision to preserve island communities, which is a passion we pursued for more than 30 years. During this time I was fortunate to be able to regularly travel the islands as part of my job, always with a camera at my side, always documenting the people, the islands. When we started the Institute, neither Philip nor I had ever asked anybody for money ever in our lives. I had the clothes on my back and a camera. That was it. We grew the Institute and it was successful. We were embraced by a lot of people out on the islands and the institute continues to make a positive impact. It was great, however it started to weigh on me and I started to feel the stress.

On January 26th, 2009 Andy died. I went down to Chadds Ford right away. It was a very sad time, and one of great reflection. One day, as I was driving back to Maine on the New Jersey Turnpike this voice in my head repeated words my father said before he died... If not now, when? You know that couplet? If not now, when? Those words meant I had done 30 years of work with Philip to build and to grow the Island Institute and to do everything that we purported to do in our mission. And we'd been very successful at it. But I was burned out. It was time to embrace what I really wanted to do: family, friends and my photography.

I've been so very, very lucky in my life, and now I love being here in my gallery surrounded by all of this. I can stand here at the door and look down on the most perfect small harbor in America and I can see one island and beyond that is the ocean. How insanely lucky am I? We're never going to be rich, but I am so incredibly rich I can't see straight. I have everything I've ever truly valued.

The saddest thing I can think of would be for any of us to have something to

I LITERALLY CANNOT UNDERSTAND WHAT GOES ON INSIDE OF SOMEONE WHO DOESN'T GO OUT AND EXPLORE, PUSH THEIR LIMITS, EXPERIMENT, EXPERIENCE THINGS, GIVE BACK.

offer and contribute nothing to life, to the world around us. A life lived and what do you have to show for it? A collection of watches or, you know, stuff... I don't comprehend it. I literally cannot understand what goes on inside of someone who doesn't go out and explore, push their limits, experiment, experience things, give back. What fills their lives and days? I just can't imagine. That's one of the few things I just cannot comprehend.

Andy said that I think with my lungs, which is so true. I enjoy good conversation, being with others, telling stories. Never let the truth get in the way of a good story! So I truly believe that all of us should absorb the world around us and really, really look. Don't be somebody who just sees things, but look. Look and see deeply. Listen, too. People are the most amazing, fascinating, confusing, confounding, wonderful, strangest creatures on the planet. There are stories everywhere. Listen to people's stories and explore with them. People love to be heard, you know. And live a full life every day.

TANIA AEBI

Her Experiment: Sailing Alone Around the World

Some people dream about sailing around the world. Very few people will ever do it. Tania Aebi was 18 years old when, on May 28, 1985, she boarded a 26' sloop to start her solo circumnavigation. When she arrived home two years later, she was the first American woman and youngest person to have ever achieved this extraordinary feat. As Tania shares in her book, Maiden Voyage, her father was the impetus for the journey. He once told her, "Think big! Think about the world that you will see. Think about sailing your own pretty little boat into an exotic foreign port and seeing it in a way that no Mickey Mouse tourist in a bubble-topped bus would ever see it. And this will be your job."

While Tania's story focuses on her circumnavigation, her grand experiment, this feat was comprised of many smaller ones. With every day at sea and every physical and mental challenge that presented itself, she found herself doing experiments—investing resources, such as her knowledge and physical capacity, to invent her future. Sometimes this future was moments away as she patched a leak or trimmed a sail, and at other times her destiny lie weeks ahead as she labored to cross an ocean. In every case she created and considered options, found ways to minimize danger, and conducted her experiments in a manner that took her from landfall to landfall until she finally achieved her dream.

grew up in an untraditional family. It was quirky, not cookie-cutter at all. First, my parents were Europeans who immigrated to the US when I was born, and they were both artists. They were sort of wacky. They had four kids and we lived in rural northern New Jersey. We were the outsiders. And then my parents went through a divorce with lots of high drama. We ended up in New York where I got to be a teenager, the funnest time in my life. It was great. I grew up among lots of artsy weirdos. I went to both a traditional and also a non-traditional high school. I finished a year early to get it done, out of the way.

At the same time I graduated from this alternative high school my dad bought a boat. I went with him for a year on it and fell in love with the whole way of life. We went from England to Spain and Portugal. We repaired our relationship that got pretty broken while I was going through my adolescent thing. One day, in the middle of the Atlantic he just popped the idea. He asked if I wanted to sail around the world. He said, "If I buy you a boat you can sail around the world instead of college, since that's probably more suited to your kind of personality." I was clearly not on the college path at that point. The world was huge, there were so many things I wanted to do and college wasn't on the list back then. I was open to this because I knew I wanted to travel. And because my dad told all his stories about his travels and all the things he did when he was younger. He was always brave about taking on challenges.

Everyone thought that I was crazy and he was crazier as a father suggesting this. You have to understand that I already experienced living on a boat. On a boat you have your house with you all the time. You're your own master and I loved the idea of that. Having an adventure that I was in complete control of. At first my dad didn't make it clear that I had to do the sail on my own. So it was a pretty *gradual process. It wasn't as if a light bulb went off in my head, at all. I did not say yes right away. It was something I gave a lot of thought to. Sometimes you're just driven by impulse or feeling or desire. Sometimes feeling is more important than every pro and con on a spreadsheet. It's an alien idea to me to have things in such black and white, to make decisions outside of what's unquantifiable but really important.*

" YOU DON'T GO AROUND THE WORLD. YOU END UP AROUND THE WORLD.

I didn't just leave on a totally hair-brained trip. It was something that I saw many other people doing, safely. And I was getting on a new boat with all new equipment. What's the worst that can happen? And what is the worst thing that can happen with everything you do? You can die. I'm not afraid. I don't go walk on the edge of a cliff. I'm never going to go base jumping, ever. I don't mind going to sea.

This is what I wanted to do, what I needed to do. I didn't have anything better to do at the time. I finished the sailing trip with my dad. We had all that experience at sea. I got back to New York and had friends going off to college, and my mother was dying at the time. I told her the idea and she thought it was really cool. She saw the possibility in it, too. I didn't have any better ideas. There wasn't anything that could even compare to this opportunity. I was mature or wise enough to know that I probably wasn't going to get another chance like this. I had to try.

It didn't seem like a big risk to me. If it gets bad I can quit, that was my mantra. And leaving wasn't really about going around the world, so much as to Bermuda. Leaving New York I just had to get to Bermuda. That was the end goal at that point. And then getting to St. Thomas. You don't go around the world. You end up around the world. That's how the story ends but all the pieces of it are pieces. I was just going with the flow. And you don't know where life will take you, what the end is going to be.

It's good to have a goal, but that goal can shift. It's not cut in stone. I mean I had to get back to New York, but the way of getting back changed along the way. I didn't have to follow a prescribed route. There was a route but it changed. It went with the seasons and the wind and the many people I talked to who shared knowledge along the way. You can't know the outcome until you've taken that first step and then experienced it. You can't outline the future without meeting the vagaries along the way and learning how to deal with them. It's just trusting the process like they told me at school. Trust the process, trust the process. So many people wig out and worry about the details of something up ahead but nothing's going to hit you all at once, and if it does you deal with it. You deal with things as they come. And with each thing you deal with you learn and pick up some more tools for continuing. So leaving New York I just rolled into it.

YOU CAN'T KNOW THE OUTCOME UNTIL YOU'VE TAKEN THAT FIRST STEP AND THEN EXPERIENCED IT.

I figured it out all along the way. It wasn't like I thought that I knew anything, much less everything, at the outset, but I totally trusted that I'd figure things out. What I knew at the back of my mind is that I was extremely lucky to be doing this trip. I was being handed this opportunity and to not try it or to be too scared or whatever, to not take the chance I would have regretted it for the rest of my life, for sure.

You figure things out with tools. There are all kinds of tools. In a literal sense, as I went along I was learning from other people's tool kits on their boats, how much easier it is to fix an engine if you have a socket wrench, for example. You fix everything with a tool. Discovering a socket wrench kit in Gibraltar. Getting a cordless drill. Wow! There are life tools, too. That's how I survived. For example, when I got knocked down in the Mediterranean I learned to not lay down on the job. After the knock-down I wanted to get off the boat, just wanted to be done. I arrived and just wanted to sleep. I got some sleep and realized that I wasn't done. Short of sinking I was never done. In my mind I would break things down. Fractions, I got really good at fractions. That's a psychological tool. You can always divide down things into quanta. When you're at 70% you're almost there, which is a lot different from 15%. Within that there is the "this too shall pass" knowledge which is acquired as you have more experiences and more things pass. The more things pass the more you learn that things will pass.

YOU FIGURE THINGS OUT WITH TOOLS.

How did this experiment impact my life? You know that's been a question I've thought about a long time. I'll never fully know. I always hated the whole self-evaluation thing. The book. That's one thing that I got out of it. You know what I got out of it? I've never had to prove myself again in such a big way. I did this trip, wrote the book and I could go on and live life without that angst of not having proven myself. I could be a totally present mother and wife. I didn't feel the pressure to be successful at anything again, other than in the short term, doing trips and taking other people sailing. Taking my kids sailing, which was my dream. In 2007 I realized that dream and took my sons

"

STEPPING OUT OF YOUR COMFORT ZONE AND INTO THE
UNKNOWN WITH JUST A GOAL OR DREAM TO CARRY YOU
ALONG IS A VULNERABLE PLACE TO BE IN, AND THAT'S
WHEN OTHERS WILL STEP UP TO SUPPORT YOU.

sailing for a year. We voyaged from the Caribbean through the Panama Canal and into the South Pacific. Any of those could have been the defining thing for me. But I had that already so there was never the pressure. That's been the long term effect on my life. I've never since felt the pressure to prove myself.

Stepping out of your comfort zone and into the unknown with just a goal or dream to carry you along is a vulnerable place to be in, and that's when others will step up to support you. It is human nature to want to help, to cheer others along. Ever since my journey, I've spent my life trying to give back in my world and to those who pass through it needing advice, an ear, some time or cheerleading, a piece of chocolate or fruitcake. This is what keeps the big wheel turning.

MARSHALL N. CARTER

His Experiment: Transforming A Bank

Growing up in a military family, it was expected that Marshall N. Carter would follow in his grandfather's and father's footsteps and join the Army. After his graduation from West Point, he rebelled and joined the Marines instead. This took him to Vietnam where he earned a Purple Heart and the prestigious Navy Cross for extraordinary heroism. He returned to the U.S. and, like many veterans, struggled to find a job. More than 80 job applications later, he was hired by a bank. Marsh went on to become Chairman and Chief Executive Officer of State Street Corporation and Executive Chairman of NYSE/Euronext, parent of the New York Stock Exchange. Since retiring, he teaches and lectures on leadership and innovation, and has continued to be a mentor to many.

Marsh offers an overview of the transformation of State Street from a regional bank into a global powerhouse. As Chairman and CEO, he led the investments that would determine the future of the company. Marsh's team cycled through many Smart Experiments: designing new service offerings, deciding which ones to pursue based on their value to the company, de-risking the company's actions through acquired experience and training, and delivering time and again. Under Marsh's leadership State Street became a leading global player and, over a 10-year period, State Street stock price increased six-fold.

When I returned from Vietnam it wasn't easy to find a job, but I got hired by Chase Manhattan Bank in New York. Starting out after several years in the military, I was older than my peers. But I had an advantage. I had leadership experience. There's a lot to be said for military training and learning to lead from the front. This means walking around and getting to know your team, the people you're working with and who depend on one another. In Vietnam we had to worry about real bullets, so to some extent the transition to the corporate world and its 'paper bullets' was easy for me. In other ways, not so easy.

At Chase I rose up through the ranks but eventually felt that I'd hit a wall. I had asked my boss for money to invest in technology and he said "No." Back then, banks didn't think much of computers because they didn't see themselves as technology companies. For several reasons I saw the world differently.

I arrived at State Street as Chairman and CEO in the summer of '91. Out of the 8,000 employees at the time, I knew two of them. So my work was cut out for me. I did a lot of walking around, visiting our facilities and talking to people. I remember visiting one of our transaction processing centers only to find that everyone was doing the accounting by hand, writing numbers in these leather-bound ledger books. They couldn't buy the quill pens any more, yet they were still doing it all by hand. Clearly it was time to bring the business into the modern age.

Behold the turtle, who gets nowhere unless his neck is stuck out. We needed to do something drastic. Not only because it was the way the world was going, but because our backs were to the wall. We had seen a 60% price erosion in our main product over 18 months. We needed to do something. In fact, the biggest *risk to our business and employees would have been to stand still. There were 25 other banks competing by buying up market share with low prices so the current business wasn't sustainable. We needed to find a way forward.*

> **❝**
>
> **BEHOLD THE TURTLE, WHO GETS NOWHERE UNLESS HIS NECK IS STUCK OUT.**

My mandate was to turn the company into a global business services firm. The way we'd do this was by growing revenue from selling value-added services to institutional investors around the world such as pension funds and mutual funds. Our goal in the 1990's was to move up the food chain and expand our services to include much higher-value offerings. We set out to empower our customers to better manage and invest their funds. It was a big global opportunity.

Two trends guided us. Global demographics told us that populations around the world were aging and there was also huge growth in investable assets. Plus the market in the Unites States was maturing. We needed international growth.

Flying back from Brussels one time I invented this thing I called the Egg Chart. It got that name just because it's a big oval I drew on a piece of paper. We didn't hire consultants or else it would have some fancy name. In any case, it was a diagram that outlined the investment process in 19 steps along with specific service offerings. It gave us a way to visualize all of our opportunities by seeing, in one place, the things money managers do and the services we could offer at each step along the way. The Egg Chart was a pictorial representation of our strategy. You've got to tell people what you're expecting them to do, what needs to be done. And you can't do that with ten pages of text.

We divided the opportunities into tactical and strategic projects. Tactical projects were short-term, usually within the next 12-18 months, and they were meant to continue and grow our existing revenue streams. We'd do this by cross-selling, reengineering things, development, adding value to existing products. Strategic projects were the bigger ideas that were going to take more time. For example, we started investing in the Internet, which was a big deal back then due to security concerns. Within five years 43% of our revenue was coming from products that didn't exist five years earlier. That's innovation at work.

Making decisions about which opportunities to fund, and how much support to put behind them, was the hardest part. But it all comes down to quantified common sense. The goals were always product profitability and growth. So I'd press my team to back up their assumptions on product values, profitability projections, market share and costs. And I would really press them hard and ask them to take me through the accounts in detail, expense and revenue, dollar by dollar. If we invest our money in one side of the box, what's coming out the other side? That's how we made the decisions.

IT ALL COMES DOWN TO QUANTIFIED COMMON SENSE.

Company culture also has a big effect on the decisions you make, meaning what people are used to and what they're open to and capable of. You know the story about Newton's First Law? A body in motion stays in motion in its original direction until you strike it smartly in the head! It's too easy for leadership to push an organization to change too quickly, and this can be counterproductive. You have to take time to convince the people who are resisting that change is irresistible.

The best way to prepare is to have the right resources, especially a well-trained team. It was true in the military and it's just as true in the corporate world. At State Street we had a great human resources group that knew how to hire well and we developed our people. I also subscribed to the idea that a leader should be surrounded by people who are going to honestly say it like it is, and not subscribe to something I call malicious obedience.

Executing our strategy, the 'real work' that followed our decisions about where to invest, included making our existing products better, building new products, cutting costs, and cross-selling. We wanted to sell a mix of between 12-15 value-added products to each of our customers.

> **THE BEST WAY TO PREPARE IS TO HAVE THE RIGHT RESOURCES.**

Our strategy paid off and State Street expanded from 1991-2001. We went from 8,000 people to over 22,000, grew our assets under custody from $498 billion to over $6 trillion, increased revenues from $792 million to $3.6 billion and our earnings from $0.78 to $3.63 per share. In 2001 we had customers in over 90 countries.

Having a sensible and clear strategy was critical. And a key for me was to lead from the front, including actively getting involved with our major clients. It's a team effort and having an exceptional team—one that knows how to get things done efficiently and effectively—makes all the difference.

Careers are long journeys, especially for young people today. Take chances and step outside of your comfort zone. Volunteer for hard jobs and travel to gain international experience. And most of all, relax and do what you love.

ELISE GOLD

Her Experiment: Starting Companies

Elise Gold* spends her days seeking to turn uncertainty into certainty—the essence of entrepreneurship—through the use of Smart Experiments. Like the rest of us, some of her experiments have resulted in better outcomes than others. A wonderful thing about Elise is that she acknowledges and shares her failures, and sees the extraordinary value in them. In fact, the reason I chose to profile her is because so few entrepreneurs and investors stand out for their grace in both failure and success. They are truly few and far between.

As an entrepreneur living in Australia, Elise has started two ventures with her husband, Dan. She thinks deeply about the process of launching businesses, if only because she's learned about entrepreneurship first-hand, through her own experiments and by experiencing the ups and downs that accompany this life. Startups offer a roller coaster ride of emotions and a sure-fire way to learn and grow. More recently, Elise has become an investor who uses her knowledge to help others pursue their dreams. As you read Elise's words you will detect an analytical mind, strong desire for meaningful pursuits, and healthy skepticism— all hallmarks of people who do Smart Experiments well.

*No relation to the author

My parents both had very challenging childhoods. *My mom's parents died when she was only 13 and she went on to become a doctor, something very rare for a woman at that time. My dad grew up in a village in northern Ghana and worked his way to come to Australia to become a dentist. So I grew up with parents who were role models. I got a sense of what it was like to work hard and always keep this at the back of my mind. Perhaps that's why I like to do things that are really hard. At university, I earned a dual degree in commerce and law. Then I began my career in investment banking. But when I met my husband, Dan, we'd visit his family and they'd sit around the table talking about new business ideas. It was all very exciting, the possibility to create something of our own.*

Dan and I decided that we needed to do something entrepreneurial together. This was an exciting time because online retail was really taking off in the U.S. and we felt the same opportunities existed in Australia. We're not a huge country so we were looking for a big market here, not just a niche. We came up with a bunch of experiments. We were looking for one that would have significant potential and that we

IT WAS ALL VERY EXCITING, THE POSSIBILITY TO CREATE SOMETHING OF OUR OWN.

could afford to pursue. After a lot of research we decided to create a daily deals website for new moms. We launched the business and it got off to a decent start. Five months later, Australia's largest online retailer approached us to talk. They knew we were onto something. At first we weren't sure of their motives, but we got to know one another and a few months after that they acquired us. Dan and I worked under them, running and growing the business we started, for 18 months. Then we left to start our next adventure.

First we needed to take a break and give it thought. There was a lot we got out of this first experience, more than just money. We enjoyed ourselves and were feeling quite optimistic. That said, we learned about the challenges of online retail and decided that our next business venture would be something completely different. At the time, we identified that food service could be a great opportunity in Australia. Many new restaurant concepts were taking off in the States and we thought we might be able to do one of these in our own way here in Australia. So we decided to make a trip to the U.S. and Italy. We visited Los Angeles, Seattle, Phoenix and Atlanta, and then flew to Naples, Italy where we took a course in pizza making at the Vera Pizza Napoletana. It was a wonderful experience but also so chauvinistic. I did well in the course and after all of the hard work my final evaluation proclaimed, "Someday you'll be a very beautiful pizza maker!"

We returned to Australia with a renewed sense of purpose and appreciation for high quality pizza. We considered a few options but most of them got eliminated quickly. Dan and I decided we wanted to experiment with something new that could reach a broad audience. Of course the economics had to work, too. Also, we wanted to invest our own time and money into something meaningful to us. We decided to try a fast casual pizzeria concept that would use healthy ingredients. It didn't exist in Australia. We called our company Melt. We didn't just jump into it. We prepared by asking lots of questions and doing our best to get answers. There were many risks we needed to pay attention to. Where should I begin? Melbourne is one of the most discerning dining scenes anywhere and people might not like our concept. Of course we intended to be different and therefore had no idea how people would respond. We also realized

"

WE WANTED TO EXPERIMENT WITH SOMETHING NEW

that to make pizza with great ingredients in a fast casual setting we'd need a location with lots of foot traffic. So our costs were high for ingredients, rent and labor, which meant we needed to serve lunch and dinner to make it work. Also, we weren't going to pay our workers under the table, which meant our labor costs were higher. We prepared by building financial models and speaking with everyone we knew in the industry. Of course we had also learned how to make great pizzas ourselves including time behind the counter. So we felt prepared to make and deliver the product. The big uncertainties were about marketing and getting customers in the door and enjoying our product, but we thought that if we did something unique we'd get customers and press.

WE ALWAYS SAY, NO, NO, WE DID FAIL!

Before launching we looked at a lot of locations and settled on an existing pizza shop. So our launch was actually running the existing business for three months to learn and get our ducks in a row. After that we sought investment and formally launched Melt. To be honest, from these early days I had a bad feeling. We were working more than 100 hours a week and it was a bigger commitment than either of us expected. Lots of things went wrong and we did our best to fix them. But we couldn't keep up. Despite our efforts, the business didn't work and we shut it down in close consultation with our investors. We lost most of our savings, and our investors' money. Nothing could have felt worse. At least our employees were able to get other jobs.

We're very open and honest about it. Whenever we tell someone that we failed, most of the time they try to reframe it, to say that we didn't really fail. We always say, NO, NO, WE DID FAIL! Failure is a source of great shame in Australia.

Despite the stigma, that's not something that bothers me or Dan. Many positives flowed from the experience. I gained incredible insight. I learned how to endure. Now I feel a lot stronger. My perspective changed. I'm more inquisitive now and extremely conscious of risks. I ask more questions that challenge assumptions. The experience magnified my respect for entrepreneurs and led to my current situation. It's so hard to do something new and make a buck in this world. Despite the business failure the experience took me to a better place. So yes, we failed, but we gained so much. I actually feel much better off.

Throughout the process, we made it a point to be completely open with our investors. They got a clear sense of how hard we were working to fix problems, and I think they came to believe in both Dan and me more than ever. When Melt failed, I immediately got a call offering me a job. About three months later one of our investors introduced me to my current situation. Amazingly, I get to leverage everything I've learned as an entrepreneur starting and running my own ventures to now help other entrepreneurs and their ventures succeed.

"

THE EXPERIENCE TOOK ME TO A BETTER PLACE.

You asked about our experiments and we were doing them all the time. We still are. It's what entrepreneurs do. Perhaps all of us. After all, the experiments we do in life are what make our lives interesting. Sometimes they pay off and at other times they don't, and I'm not just talking about finances. Money is important, but only as a lifeblood that keeps you in business. Success in my mind is about being satisfied with my lot. If I'm sensible and give it my all, then I'm content. Success means waking up excited every morning. What more could you ask for?

FIVE LESSONS

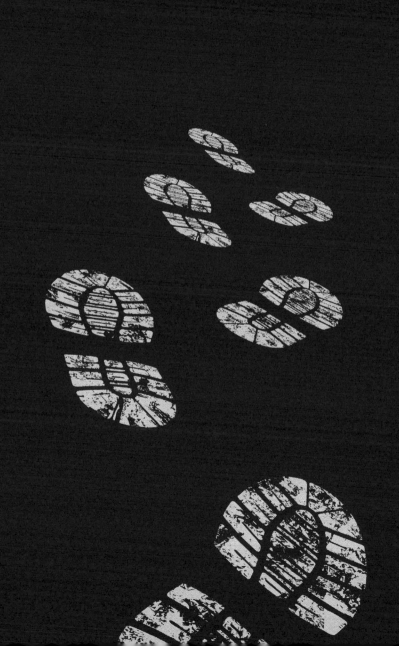

1. Start by starting—and keep going!

Sometimes we need a reminder or even a swift kick in the pants! If we see that we need to *take action* to succeed, then starting is the first key to succeeding.

The single best way to accumulate more and more value over time is to re-invest the value that we already possess—our available resources—to do Smart Experiments. By taking this approach, we increase our chances of ending up with more value than we started with following every Smart Experiment we do. There will of course be many bumps in the road, and even roadblocks, but the Smart Experiment process works beautifully over the long run.

The highest achievers are always doing Smart Experiments and they don't let their available resources stand idle. They feel compelled to take action, to do a Smart Experiment, and frequently several Smart Experiments simultaneously. All of this starts with self-drive and the determination to get going.

Despite the obvious point that everything depends on a beginning, there are many individuals and organizations who are paralyzed and don't take this first step. Instead, they hoard the value that they have, in spite of the clear evidence that stored value degrades over time. Physical things can deteriorate or get rusty. People's emotions change. They may be a best friend one moment and not have time to speak with you the next. Even idle cash is perishable as the forces of inflation and opportunity cost eat away at it. There are no excuses and only one thing to do: get going! And then...

Just do It

Nike

Keep going! Everything depends on taking a next step.

We've come this far and the last thing we want to do now is stop at the end of any Smart Experiment. As we now know, a smart investment of value leads to the accumulation of more value, and doing nothing only leads to nothing (or worse) as value perishes over time. With this in mind, the clear strategy is to be actively investing value and doing one Smart Experiments after the next.

The drawing on the next page represents a concept that I call the Success Spiral. Every time we conduct another Smart Experiment we take another turn around the spiral. By continuously cycling through Smart Experiments—doing one experiment after the next and even several at a time—we build up more and more value. We invest, harvest, reinvest and repeat the process. The smarter we do each experiment, the faster we cycle around the Success Spiral and accumulate more value. Even if an experiment leads to the loss of some value, that's OK. It's all part of the plan, so long as we can continue and do our next Smart Experiment, and then the next one, spiraling upward.

★

GET GOING
AND KEEP
GOING.

Experiment after experiment, cycle after cycle, the net effect is that we're able to compound, so to speak, value over time. We start with X, build it up over our first several Smart Experiments, and ultimately get to 10X or 100X or more.

The bottom line is that Smart Experiments work provided that we do them well and keep on doing them. So whether we're interested in them for personal reasons or for the benefit of our teams and organizations (or both), the first and most important lesson is clear—start now and keep going.

2. Take smaller steps for bigger progress

Experiments can—and often should—be broken down into smaller pieces. This allows us to accumulate value more quickly. The idea here is to do the smallest experiment that's likely to lead to a meaningful result. In other words, instead of betting the whole farm, bet only a small part of the farm at a time.

By doing smaller experiments we:

- **Lower potential loss.** The immediate implication of doing things in smaller steps is that the possible loss of value for each experiment is much lower than the possible downside for a bigger experiment. If something goes wrong, as is frequently the case, we hold onto more resources to invest in the future. Smaller experiments are safer experiments.

- **Stay flexible.** We all fear commitment because the future is so uncertain. Consider walking across an unfamiliar room in total darkness. Experiments are like that. The smart approach is to take small steps and feel our way along. As we encounter obstacles, we change our course to avoid them. Flexibility and reduced commitment also help motivate us to get started.

- **Gain efficiency.** During a family trip to our nation's capital, I was walking fast with our young daughter tired and lagging behind me. At one point, I walked in the wrong direction for about five minutes before noticing my mistake. She told me, "Daddy, if you walked slower, we would have gotten there a lot faster." Smaller steps allow us to point ourselves in the right direction a lot faster.

It's possible to take a smaller step at virtually any time by considering that all of our past experiences have delivered us to the present moment. This frees us to ask ourselves, "What is the Smart Experiment that we will do *starting now*?"

GREAT THINGS ARE NOT DONE BY
IMPULSE, BUT BY A SERIES OF
SMALL THINGS BROUGHT TOGETHER.

Vincent van Gogh

3. Failing is essential to succeeding

This is something we need to consider, as individuals and as a society.

Failing is a necessary and inevitable part of succeeding. If we wish to achieve anything truly meaningful in our lives, it will at times involve sticking our necks out and taking risks. The objective is not to avoid taking risks, but rather to be smart about taking them—to be sure that every experiment is meaningful, that it doesn't risk everything and prevent us from doing our next experiment if it fails, that we're prepared for the things that are most likely to go wrong, and more. In other words we're giving it our best and doing Smart Experiments.

Many successful people talk about the importance of taking risks and that failing turned out to be so wonderful for them, etc. The concept that failing is part of succeeding is easy for people to talk about after they've achieved success and have discretionary resources that are easier for them to place at risk. I get this. But all of us need to think deeply about how failing fits into our lives. In my research, I've found that a high tolerance for failing is causative for succeeding much more consistently over the long-term. Successful people fail more (and bigger) and they accept that this is an integral part of the process. Conversely, a low tolerance for failure implies lower achievement. This is because most people with a low tolerance for risk avoid doing things. Since everything has at least some element of risk, they mitigate their risks by doing less, and the result is that they acquire much less value over time due to the compounding effect.

The idea that failing has benefits is a paradox. But it's also an inevitable conclusion. Failing more is an essential part of succeeding more over the long run.

FAILURE IS A MANIFESTATION
OF LEARNING AND EXPLORATION.
IF YOU AREN'T EXPERIENCING FAILURE,
THEN YOU ARE MAKING A FAR WORSE MISTAKE:
YOU ARE BEING DRIVEN BY THE DESIRE TO AVOID IT.

Ed Catmull

4. Celebrate effort instead of outcomes

We all need to resist the urge to celebrate success and punish failure—for others and ourselves. The evidence tells us that we should celebrate intelligent effort through incentives, rewards and reinforcement. Another way to say this is that we want to celebrate our Smart Experiments and not their outcomes.

Why celebrate Smart Experiments irrespective of outcome? First, many of our perceived successes are due to copious amounts of luck—being in the right place at the right time, for example. When we celebrate what is frequently just luck, we reinforce the wrong individual and organizational priority.

Think about a time you've had a successful outcome and been rewarded. Then think about another time when the outcome wasn't successful, despite having worked even smarter and harder, and you were punished for it. This kind of response—by bosses, colleagues and ourselves—prioritizes luck over effort and discourages all of us from doing the right things and improving ourselves. It's a plague that encourages laziness (why work hard if we're just being rewarded for luck?) and leads to poor performance by both people and organizations.

Why would we punish or ignore behavior that we want to reinforce? Instead, let's take the time to encourage the behavior that best correlates with success and the accumulation of value over time—doing Smart Experiments.

Top achievers obsessively focus on the future and making good things happen. They prize intelligent effort over luck because it works over the long run.

Let's celebrate our Smart Experiments!

MY DAD ENCOURAGED US TO FAIL. GROWING UP, HE WOULD ASK US WHAT WE FAILED AT THAT WEEK. IF WE DIDN'T HAVE SOMETHING, HE WOULD BE DISAPPOINTED. IT CHANGED MY MINDSET AT AN EARLY AGE THAT FAILURE IS NOT THE OUTCOME—FAILURE IS NOT TRYING.

Sara Blakely

5. Empower others

One of the most gratifying aspects of my life is being able to help others—young entrepreneurs, executives, young people—to achieve more in their lives.

Over the years, this has provided many memorable moments and meaningful rewards. It's always wonderful to learn that someone has benefited from an understanding of Smart Experiments and how to do them well.

Another benefit that surprised me at first, is that by empowering other people with the ability to do Smart Experiments, we expand our networks of relationships with people who are themselves investing their resources wisely and achieving great things. In this synergistic twist, by surrounding ourselves with others who are achieving and succeeding more, we open up a new universe of possibilities for ourselves. This is a big part of the Success Spiral I described earlier.

So find ways to empower your family members, friends, team members and entire organizations with Smart Experiments. Spread the idea, in your own way. Nothing says it more powerfully than if each of us walks the walk and practices what we preach by using Smart Experiments and sharing the rewards.

REAL GENEROSITY TOWARD THE FUTURE LIES
IN GIVING ALL TO THE PRESENT.

Albert Camus

RESOURCES

Selected resources

These books and articles relate to Smart Experiments, offering insights and ideas to help us do them well (listed alphabetically by title):

Creativity, Inc.: Overcoming the Unseen Forces That Stand in the Way of True Inspiration by Ed Catmull, the title says it all. Random House, 2014.

Drive: The Surprising Truth About What Motivates Us by Daniel Pink, talks about Autonomy, Mastery and Purpose. Riverhead Books, 2011

The Entrepreneur's Manual by Richard White, is brilliant but out of print so get a copy if you're lucky to find one. Chilton Book, 1977.

Getting There: A Book of Mentors by Gillian Zoe Segal offers a wonderful collection of personal stories and wisdom. Harry N. Abrams, 2015.

Influence: The Psychology of Persuasion by Robert Cialdini, provides great insight about what moves us. Harper Business, 2006.

Just Start: Take Action, Embrace Uncertainty, Create the Future by Leonard Schlesinger, et al., says action trumps all. HBR Press, 2012.

Learning Through Failure: The Strategy of Small Losses by Sim Sitkin, Research in Organizational Behavior, Volume 14, pages 231-266, 1992.

Mindset: The New Psychology of Success by Carol Dweck, shares her work about why effort matters most. Random House, 2006.

Small Wins: Redefining the Scale of Social Problems by Karl Weick, is about approaching larger challenges. American Psychologist, 1984.

Here are some of my favorite books about real and fictional people, and how experiments, relationships and expertise are used to invent the future:

Adventures of Huckleberry Finn by Mark Twain, the ingenious novel that epitomizes a life of exploration. Various, originally published in 1884.

The First Tycoon: The Epic Life of Cornelius Vanderbilt by T.J. Stiles, is one of the best written biographies I've ever read. Vintage Press, 2010.

The Last Lion, three book series by William Manchester, tells the saga of Winston Churchill and his fascinating life. Little Brown & Co., 2012.

The Path Between the Seas: The Creation of the Panama Canal by David McCullough, shares this grand experiment. Simon & Schuster, 1977.

Rocket Boys: A Memoir by Homer Hickam, the autobiography behind the inspirational movie *October Sky*. Island Books, 2001.

Ship of Gold in the Deep Blue Sea: History and Discovery of the World's Richest Shipwreck by Gary Kinder, a tale of two experiments. Grove Press, 2009.

Videos are an incredible way to learn. Here are a few that I especially enjoy for their insights and inspirational value. They are easy to find online:

Steve Jobs 2005 Stanford University Commencement Speech

J.K. Rowling 2008 Harvard University Commencement Speech

Randy Pausch Lecture "Achieving Your Childhood Dreams"

Tony Robbins TED Talk "Why We Do What We Do"

J.J. Abrams TED Talk "The Mystery Box"

Acknowledgments

We all stand on the shoulders of giants. I am incredibly fortunate in my life to have the love, support and encouragement of many people whom I respect and admire. While the words in this book are mine, the lessons are theirs.

My family is first on the list for their total love and support of all my adventures (and misadventures), and for joining right in. Not every parent is willing to let their son fly and sail off into the horizon, and not every spouse is willing to pack up and move the family to Borneo on three weeks notice. And seeing my kids do Smart Experiments in pursuit of their own dreams is my dream come true.

Next up are those individuals who have believed in me and opened doors. I'm indebted to Richard Miller and Michael Moody of Franklin W. Olin College and Leonard Schlesinger of Babson College and Harvard Business School. Special thanks also go to Edward Beiser and Philip Maddock of Brown Medical School. Marshall N. Carter and George Stevens, both officers and gentlemen, epitomize generosity and serve as my role models for what every leader should be.

I am grateful to many friends from around the globe: Zulkarnain Hanafi, Anita Aziz, Joyce Teo, Najwa Majid, Adna Rahman, Jorg Jacobsen, Keith Miller, Derek Browne, Paul Booth, Robert Plotkin, Peter Ralston, Mark Sklar, Dan & Elise Gold—all of whom embody endless enthusiasm and entrepreneurial energy.

Last but not least, several exceptional professionals have brought this book to life. They include talented artists Carol Fazio, Albert Ganss, Mihaela Drakulovic and Andrew Lee. Lots of editing and other valuable feedback were thoughtfully provided by my friends Stephen Meuse and Christine Alaimo. Thank you all!

A. Ganss

About the author

Steven K. Gold empowers individuals and organizations using the lessons of entrepreneurial strategy and practice. As Chairman of Gold Global Advisors, he advises clients throughout the United States, Europe, Middle East and Asia.

Steve began his career as an entrepreneur who started and successfully exited several ventures in the fields of biotechnology, software, mobile mapping and intellectual property. He was then invited to teach entrepreneurship, first as Senior Partner for Entrepreneurship at Franklin W. Olin College of Engineering, and later as Professor of Entrepreneurship Practice at Babson Global. Steve has taught entrepreneurial strategy and practice to audiences around the world.

Steve is the inventor on ten issued patents, and author of *Entrepreneur's Notebook: Practical Advice for Starting a New Business Venture* and *How We Succeed: Making Good Things Happen through the Power of Smart Experiments*. He's an expert on the behavioral science of sustainable success. He helps leaders and organizations of all kinds compete most effectively in today's global environment.

Steve is a graduate of the Wharton School of the University of Pennsylvania and Brown University Medical School. He's also completed Harvard Law School's Program on Negotiation. Steve and his family live in Lexington, Massachusetts.

www.stevenkgold.com